AF374818

Title: Me amo

Sub - Title: Love Yourself Immensely

By: Dr. Roberto Jimenez

Design: Smartners Business Services

Copy Right: ©Roberto Jimenez

First Print: December 2022

Description

This book introduces readers to self-love and its relation to physical and psychosocial well-being. The book's primary aim is to impart knowledge on self-love to promote positive behavioral and cognitive patterns, ensuring mental well-being and a positive perception of self. The book contains a step-by-step structure with seven lessons, each tackling a critical aspect of self-love, from its definition to its relation to psychotherapeutic approaches.

About the
Author

Roberto is a Licensed **Marriage & Family Therapist** in Florida, a Licensed Mental Health Counselor in Florida, an Independent Marriage & Family Therapist in Ohio, a Licensed Professional Counselor in Puerto Rico, a Licensed Marriage & Family Therapist in North Carolina and a Certified Telehealth Practitioner.

Self-Love:
Meaning, Importance, and How to Achieve It

Introduction

This book introduces the readers to the concept of self-love and its relation to physical and psychosocial well-being. The book's primary aim is to impart knowledge on self-love to promote positive behavioral and cognitive patterns, ensuring mental well-being and a positive perception of self.

The book contains a step-by-step structure with seven lessons, each tackling a critical aspect of self-love, from its definition to its relation to psychotherapeutic approaches. The book also caters to all types of readers, including visual, auditory, kinesthetic, reading, and writing, providing different activities that promote comprehension. The content also relies on simplified language to promote ease of understanding. Each of the seven topics will take 40 minutes, with an assessment at the end of the session. The book outline below provides details on the content and structure.

Book Outline

Content Goals

By the end of this book, you will be able to:

1. Define self-love and outline its fundamental components

2. Demonstrate an understanding of the relationship between self-love and health

3. Identify factors and behaviors that reduce or prevent self-love

4. Employ different evidence-based approaches to evaluate and improve self-love

5. Describe the role of psychotherapy in improving self-love

Topics

1.Introduction to self-love

a. Definition of self-love

b. The mind

c. The body

d. The spirit

e. Assessment

2. Elements of self-love

a. Self-awareness

b. Self-worth

c. Self-esteem

d. Self-worth

e. Assessment

3. Importance of self-love

a. Self-love and mental well-being

b. Self-love and physical well-being

c. Self-love and social well-being

d. Assessment

4. Threats to self-love

a. Conflicting needs

b. Poor social support

c. Lack of resources

d. Assessment

a. Improving total health

b. Psychotherapy

c. Assessment

Introduction to Self-Love

Objectives

- To define the meaning of self-love and its constituent elements
- To describe behavior that exhibits self-love

Definition of Self love

In this part, we shall define the meaning of self-love and consequently apply the definition to identify behavior or thoughts that amount to self-love. Although the term seems self-explanatory, many people do not understand what it entails and its distinction from selfishness or egocentrism. Unlike selfishness and egocentrism, self-love is an umbrella word that defines caring for oneself without harming others. According to Knox (2018), self-love refers to self-appreciation, a product of spiritual, psychological, and physical growth.

Self-love means being concerned and actively promoting happiness and general well-being. Thus, it focuses on a person's physical, psychological, emotional, and social well-being. However, this well-being does not come at the expense of other people's well-being. It stems from prioritizing self to the necessary extent that sustains total health. The three mentioned areas: spiritual, physical, and psychological, are essential for self-love. The spiritual self refers to one's sense of purpose and meaning in their life. It can derive from culture and beliefs in many areas, including religion.

On the other hand, the physical self refers to the body and its health. The psychological self refers to mental and emotional well-being. Generally, self-love is a holistic concept that promotes self-care to improve health outcomes.

Learning Activities

1 Use the definition described to discuss and identify which of the following behaviors are not demonstrations of self-love.

a. Cosmetic surgery to gain social media followers

b. Dieting to prevent health problems

c. Refusing to go out with friends because of being worn out

d. Ending social relationships for being emotionally abusive

e. Using vengeance to address feelings of hurt in a relationship

Learning Assessment Questions

Answer the following questions:

a. Briefly define self-love.
b. Provide five examples of behaviors that depict self-love.

RJIMENEZ
COUNSELING

I LOVE
ALL OF
me

Elements of
Self-Love

Objectives

- To identify and define the core aspects of self-love

- To understand how these aspects interact and interdepend on well-being
This topic explores the core components of self-love.

As noted in the previous lesson, self-love is an umbrella term comprising other elements that are products of intrinsic and extrinsic factors. Mental health, in particular, is critical for self-love. Accordingly, four main aspects emerge, which interact to produce self-love. Any challenges in one of these aspects, including self-esteem, self-worth, self-awareness, and self-care, will impede self-love and vice versa.

Self - Worth

Self-worth is a critical psychosocial phenomenon that refers to the level of self-belief. According to Soares et al. (2022), self-worth means the innate sense of being sufficiently good and deserving belonging and love from self and others.

Self-worth denotes how people value themselves in any context. However, a critical factor in defining self-worth is its intrinsic characteristic.

Topic 2

 Notably, it is not how one perceives their environment's opinion or valuation of them but how they view themselves. Although the two are related, self-worth is different. For example, a person with a high sense of self-worth will have confidence in their ability to succeed in a specific skill, course, or career without relying on external reinforcement. However, a person with a lower sense of self-worth will severely doubt their capability even when they have the necessary qualifications and strengths. Therefore, self-worth has close connections to aspects such as confidence and self-belief.

These definitions highlight the self-love-self-worth relationship. High self-worth often corresponds to self-love. Soares et al. (2022) assert that low self-worth develops from emotional and psychological challenges and may indicate mental health issues. In contrast, self-love fosters general health and well-being, including in the psycho-emotional areas. Notably, poor self-worth severely hinders performance in many areas of life, such as social relationships. Thus, one has to improve their sense of self-worth to attain self-love.

Self - Esteem

Self-esteem is also a core aspect of self-love and is closely related to self-worth. Soares et al. (2022) define self-esteem as a person's overall evaluation of their value. Therefore, it comprises the intrinsic aspects of self-worth and the external environment. While self-worth reflects a personal perspective of one's value, self-esteem reflects their views on how the external environment perceives them. Therefore, self-esteem is, to a great extent, a product of self-worth.

A person with a high sense of self-worth is likely to have correspondingly high self-esteem, while low self-worth negatively impacts self-esteem. The manifestation of self-esteem affects behavioral or character traits, including confidence. Poor self-esteem hinders a person's ability to perform in several areas of life because they do not have the necessary confidence and self-worth.

Self Love
is Your
Super
Power

RJIMENEZ
COUNSELING

Consequently, they may suffer from an inferiority complex and have self-doubt that stops them from performing. Self-love and self-esteem are interdependent. Self-love promotes psychosocial and physical well-being that provides self-confidence, ultimately boosting self-esteem. Therefore, one cannot have self-esteem without self-love and vice versa.

Self - Awareness

Self-awareness is also a critical aspect of self-love. According to Soares et al. (2022), self-awareness is a person's ability to focus on their thoughts, actions, and emotions and compare them to internal standards. It is the capacity to identify thought processes and their relations to actions and emotions.

Self-aware persons can identify specific thoughts that make them have emotions and recognize how they influence their behaviors.

This process underlies critical competencies such as emotional intelligence, which promotes effective social interactions. The ability that comes with self-awareness ultimately allows individuals to isolate their thoughts and control them effectively to promote well-being (Soares et al., 2022). For instance, a stressed, self-aware person can know whether work or personal relationships cause the underlying thoughts that make them feel stressed and act similarly.

Topic 2

The relationship between self-love and self-awareness is interdependence. Self-awareness enables an individual to identify the causes of negative thoughts and emotions and their resulting negative behaviors to avoid them, thereby promoting well-being. This process is in line with the definition of self-love. Therefore, self-awareness remains a critical aspect of self-love.

Topic 2

Self - Care

This final aspect of self-love is fundamental for well-being. As the term suggests, it refers to providing sufficient attention to one's well-being needs, including the physical, psychological, and social (Soares et al., 2022). Thus, self-care means any action that identifies and works towards meeting needs of all types. Physically, eating a proper diet to reduce weight and attain an average body mass index is an example of self-care. Socially, an example of self-care includes getting rid of toxic friends or relationships that do not support one's progress and emotional well-being. Psychologically, using different approaches to reduce stress, such as meditation and avoiding stressors, are examples of self-care activities.

Therefore, similar to self-awareness, self-care is a process of self-love because it promotes overall well-being and development in all areas of health. Along with the other three, these aspects contribute to self-love, with the lack of one affecting all the others, leading to adverse mental, psychological, and social well-being outcomes and impeding personal development.

Learning Assessment Questions

a. Briefly explain the difference between self-worth and self-esteem and their relationship with self-love.

b. How does poor self-awareness affect self-love?

c. List and explain at least five actions you have ever taken that demonstrate self-care

Importance of **Self-Love**

Objectives

- Explain how self-love affects physical health

- Explain how self-love affects mental health

- Explain how self-love affects mental health

- Explain how self-love affects social well-being

Self-Love and Mental Wellbeing

This topic will focus on justifications of self-love and how its core aspects contribute to well-being in all aspects of health. All self-love aspects defined in the previous lesson impact mental health. Mental health covers psychological, emotional, and social aspects of well-being (Soares et al., 2022).

People that can effectively cope with life challenges and maintain appropriate cognitive and thought processes that support their development and normal functioning are mentally healthy.

Topic 3

Therefore, poor mental health hinders this progress and functioning. Related conditions and disorders like depression, anxiety, and borderline personality disorder affect thoughts and behaviors. They can lead to self-harming tendencies and poor coping strategies, such as substance abuse and suicidal ideations (Hansson et al., 2020). Mental illness also impedes cognitive functions, including learning and concentration, leading to far-reaching implications.

Hence, since poor mental health risks physical and social well-being, self-love is necessary to prevent these outcomes. Individuals can improve their mental well-being through self-awareness and self-care as part of self-love to promote their overall well-being.
Self-Love and Physical Well-being is also a core component of general health, making self-love necessary to improve it.

Topic 3

Physical health is a basic need for human survival and functioning. Some numerous illnesses and conditions can impede normal functioning and threaten human life. Notably, lifestyle diseases resulting from human behavior and habits are increasingly becoming major public health issues.

They are leading causes of death and reasons for increased healthcare costs that burden individuals and societies (Anderson & Durstine, 2019). Self-love promotes total health and well-being and identifies the consequences of actions and decisions concerning physical well-being. Dieting and exercising to keep fit and avoiding harmful habits such as excessive alcohol consumption and tobacco smoking are measures that promote physical health. They demonstrate self-care, which is a critical aspect of self-love. They justify the significance of self-love.

Self-Love and Social Wellbeing

Social well-being is a product of all other aspects, including mental and physical well-being. Soares et al. (2022) define social well-being as contributing to and promoting a sense of belongingness to a society or community. It also entails sustaining relationships with other people and groups that promote personal development and support functioning. Despite this, poor mental and physical health impact social well-being, particularly in relationships and interactions. Movement restriction and other extrinsic cultural factors such as stigma and discrimination impede social functioning. Consequently, individuals cannot obtain social support and leverage social resources to promote their development and well-being.

Social well-being is a product of all other aspects, including mental and physical well-being. Soares et al. (2022) define social well-being as contributing to and promoting a sense of belongingness to a society or community. It also entails sustaining relationships with other people and groups that promote personal development and support functioning. Despite this, poor mental and physical health impact social well-being, particularly in relationships and interactions. Movement restriction and other extrinsic cultural factors such as stigma and discrimination impede social functioning. Consequently, individuals cannot obtain social support and leverage social resources to promote their development and well-being. Awareness and self-care, where a person identifies and avoids stressors and other threats to their general well-being. These functions justify the significance of self-love.

Having positive feelings about yourself maybe a crucial ingredient Happiness and Success

1 Practice self-love, self-compassion, kindness, forgiveness and self-gratitude

Learning Assessment Questions

a. Explain how self-love promotes mental, physical, and social well-being.

b. How can a general lack of self-love affect a person's health and development?

c. Describe a real or hypothetical experience where self-love promoted development and well-being.

RJIMENEZ
COUNSELING
Love
yourself

Threats and impediments of
Self - Love

Objective

- Explain how conflicting needs undermine self-love.
- Explain how social support and cultural factors affect self-love.
- Explain the role of ignorance in poor self-love
- Explain how lack of resources affects self-love.

Conflicting Needs

Conflicting needs can impede an individual's capacity for self-love. According to Kinser et al. (2021), paying attention to one's needs requires balancing other needs, including those of other people. When individuals consider others' needs more pressing, they are likely to disregard their own and focus on the other person. A typical example of needs conflict is that between mother and child. Mothers often provide most of the child care, especially during infancy (Kinser et al., 2021). Therefore, whenever a conflict arises, the mother ignores their self-care needs. The lack of time to unwind and rest leads to mental health problems such as postpartum depression.

Therefore, conflict of needs is a significant barrier to self-love. While people may be willing to care for themselves, they avoid it because they must take care of a more severe need. Poor Social Support and Related Cultural Factors Limited social support can also limit a person's capacity to provide self-love. This factor relates closely to the needs conflict because support is necessary to overcome such challenges. Women have challenges providing self-care because, in many cases, they do not get sufficient support in meeting essential responsibilities like child care (Kinser etal., 2021). Notably, cultural factors such as the patriarchal system place the domestic duties on the woman, which overwhelms many of them. Women with multiple children with insufficient support suffer mental, physical, and social challenges as they relegate their needs and interests to care for them. Therefore, without social support, providing self-love is highly challenging.

Lack of Resources

Besides needs conflict and poor social support, the inadequacy of resources impedes self-love. Knox (2018) note that self-care, a critical aspect of self-love, comes at a cost, requiring money, time, and other enabling resources like information. Thus, insufficiency makes self-love impossible. For example, healthy diets with organic food options may not be affordable to low-income households. Therefore, though they may intend to provide self-love, they are limited resource-wise. Other self-love and self-care activities require resources like time and money, making them impossible when a person cannot access them. Therefore, resources are critical external factors that impede self-love. It is also crucial to eliminate these barriers among vulnerable populations to promote well-being and better public health outcomes.

Learning Assessment Questions

a.Explain how conflicting needs impede self-love providing at least two examples.

b.How does culture affect self-love?

c.Explain with an example how resource insufficiency impedes self-love provision

RJIMENEZ
COUNSELING

Providing
Self - Love

Objectives

- Identify and explain activities that promote mental, physical, and social well-being.
- Define conditions under which a person may need psychotherapy to improve self-love
- Explain how cognitive-behavioral therapy (CBT) affects self-love.

Improving Total Health

1 Self-worth and self-esteem

1. Do not compare yourself with other people.

2. Do not worry so much about other people's opinions on personal matters such as physical appearance.

3. Mistakes are a normal part of human development

Topic 5

2 Self-awareness and self-care

1 Do not hesitate to exit toxic relationships
2 Process, understand, and overcome fears
3 Trust and have confidence in your decision making
4 Do not be afraid to take chances and utilize opportunities for personal progress.
5 Be kind in evaluating yourself.
6 Take control of your physical well-being and change harmful behaviors

Psychotherapy

Although there are many approaches to providing self-love, many people may need psychotherapeutic interventions to start or sustain the process. People with severe mental health problems do not appreciate their need for self-love and self-care because of negative thought patterns (Van Lieshout et al., 2020).

Topic 5

For instance, racism or bullying victims may feel insufficient and fail to understand how such a thought paradigm is misguided based on their bad experiences. Such people need interventions to change their cognitive patterns and positively influence their behavior. Persons with mental health challenges and severely compromised thought processes need psychotherapy to promote self-love.

CBT is highly effective for this purpose. CBT is a comprehensive approach to counseling that addresses primary and secondary problems. CBT focuses on the cognitive aspects, including the thoughts that lead to negative emotions and the behaviors resulting from the compromised decision-making process (Van Lieshout et al., 2020). CBT can address mental health patients' thought challenges and promote self-awareness, allowing them to identify and isolate negative patterns and avoid stressors. This capability makes the approach highly effective in fostering self-love and self-care in such people. In that regard, persons with mental health problems should have access to psychotherapy to promote self-care.

Learning Assessment Questions

a. Outline activities that promote self-love in all the three core areas of well-being.
b. State and explain the conditions under which a person may need psychotherapy to promote self-love.
c. How does CBT address the self-love and self-care challenges in people with mental illnesses such as depression?

RJIMENEZ
COUNSELING

Me
Amo

Accepting all of me

Self-love starts when I accept all parts of myself. Learning how to unblock our energies and allowing the colors of the seven chakras to flow freely which they say are the main energy centers of the body. We are able to reached a harmony state between the physical body, mind, and spirit. **Mantra. When I love myself, loving others comes easily.**

The Six Colors of Self-Love

GREEN - MENTAL HEALTH

We are focusing on mental health and stress management. We are incorporating new healthy habits and coping skills.

BLUE - SELF ACCEPTANCE

I am embracing every part of myself.
Self-acceptance is unconditional
Nurture your self-acceptance.

ORANGE - Self-Worth

Self-worth is the beliefs we have about ourselves.
Self-worth lies in all the good things about you. Everyone has something good about them.

Write down all of the things you have done right and include the things that other people have appreciated about you.

You are worth it regardless of your attributes or accomplishments. Your strengths, talents, and kind acts toward others are just an expression of your self-worth.

Our communication with ourselves: Quiet your inner critic by adopting a mantra ("I am doing the best I can right now").

Our communication with others impacts our self-esteem, and our self-esteem affects our communication with others. As such, our self-esteem and communication are constantly being transformed by each other.
Make sure you balance the Give and Take dance by setting healthy boundaries.

Self-care is how you care for yourself to stay physically, mentally, and emotionally well. Its benefits are better physical, mental, and emotional health and well-being. What can we do to care about our bodies, hearts, minds, and spirits?

Self-awareness is being aware of your thought processes: your thoughts, how they affect your emotions, and how emotions cause you to act. One way to improve your self-awareness is to keep a journal of your thoughts, emotions, and actions.

Mental
Health

Focusing on stress
management and
mental health. Learning
healthy coping
skills

Self
Acceptance

Accepting that you do
not have to be perfect
to be worthy
of love.

Self
Discovery

Learning your likes.
Developing goals, hobbies,
& interests that make you
happy.

Boundaries

Cultivating healthy
communication and
boundaries in your
relationships.
Give and take.

Foundations of Self / Love

Inner Voice

Changing the way you talk
to and about yourself.
Working on the voice in
your head

Self - Care

Making the time to meet
your needs as best you
can. Spending time on
your hobbies and
interests.

RJIMENEZ
COUNSELING

RJIMENEZ
COUNSELING
More SELF love
yes you can
self love

RJIMENEZ
COUNSELING
Love
Yourself
Inmensely

- Dedicated
- Creative
- Flexible
- Resourceful
- Problem-solving skills
- Ability to work under pressure
- Time management skills
- Team player
- Fast learner
- Leadership skills

- Typing skills
- Writing skills
- Determination
- Negotiation skills
- Communication skills
- Honest
- Caring
- Good listener
- Great parent
- Good daughter or son
- Terrific Brother or sister

Another ____

References

Anderson, E., & Durstine, J. L. (2019). Physical activity, exercise, and chronic diseases: A brief review. Sports Medicine and Health Science, 1(1), 3–10. https://doi.org/10.1016/j.smhs.2019.08.006

Hansson, K., Malmkvist, L., & Johansson, B. A. (2020). A 15-year follow-up of former self-harming inpatients in child & adolescent psychiatry–A qualitative study. Nordic Journal of Psychiatry, 74(4), 273–279. https://doi.org/10.1080/08039488.2019.1697747

Kinser, P. A., Jallo, N., Amstadter, A. B., Thacker, L. R., Jones, E., Moyer, S., & Salisbury, A. L. (2021). Depression, anxiety, resilience, and coping: The experience of pregnant and new mothers during the first few months of the COVID-19 pandemic. Journal of Women's Health, 30(5), 654–664. https://doi.org/10.1089/jwh.2020.8866

Knox, A. (2018). Examining self-love, love of the 'other' and love of the 'enemy': A reply to Mitchell. Global Discourse, 8(4), 610–614. https://doi.org/10.1080/23269995.2018.1530917

Soares, C. M., Leite, Â., & Pinto, M. (2022). Self-care practices with psychedelics–A qualitative study of users' perspectives. Journal of Psychoactive Drugs. Advance online publication. https://doi.org/10.1080/02791072.2022.2071134

Van Lieshout, R. J., Layton, H., Feller, A., Ferro, M. A., Biscaro, A., & Bieling, P. J. (2020). Public health nurse delivered group cognitive behavioral therapy (CBT) for postpartum depression: A pilot study. Public Health Nursing, 37(1), 50–55. https://doi.org/10.1111/phn.12664